# *Stahly Quality Foods . . .*

In the early 1900's, my Grandfather began making haggis in Dunfermline, Fife. Now in the third generation, I have taken our original highly acclaimed, award-winning recipe and packaged it in a tin to suit the ever demanding international marketplace.

I have often been asked by people from all walks of life, "What do you do with a haggis?" This was the inspiration to bring together a collection of recipes using Stahly Quality Foods tinned haggis and showing it's true potential as a very versatile dish.

Inside you will find some of our own simple family recipes which have been handed down through the generations. There are also gourmet dishes from the Executive Chefs of Scotland's top 10 hotels. I hope these will ban some of the mystery and prejudices surrounding haggis and encourage more people, including the Scots, to appreciate the versatility of Scotland's national dish.

Ken Stahly
Managing Director
Stahly Quality Foods Ltd.

HAGGIS *Recipe Book*

*A Warm Salad of Roast Scallops, with Haggis and Smoked Bacon*

# A Warm Salad of Roast Scallops, with Haggis and Smoked Bacon

## Ingredients . . .

113gms (4oz) mixed small salad leaves (baby spinach, rocquette, mizuma, red chard, endive)

18 scallops

170gms (6oz) haggis

3 rashers smoked streaky bacon

Balsamic vinegar

Salad dressing

Olive oil for frying

## Method . . .

Form haggis into small patés and pan fry on both sides. Grill bacon and reserve both in a warm place. Pan fry the scallops in a pre-heated pan, with a little olive oil; cook on one side for about 1 minute until seared then turn over and sear the other side.

To serve . . .

Dress salad and place on centre of plate. Dice slices of haggis and bacon rashers and scatter over salad and around. Place scallops on plate (3 per portion) one at the top, others bottom left and bottom right. Drizzle a little balsamic vinegar over and around scallops. Serves 6.

David Wilson Executive Chef/ Proprietor

The Peat Inn, Cupar, KY15 5LH, Scotland

Tel: +44 (0) 1334 840206 · Web: www.thepeatinn.co.uk

THE·PEAT·INN

HAGGIS Recipe Book

# HAGGIS Recipe Book

Surf & Turf with Haggis Ravioli

# Surf & Turf, with Haggis Ravioli

## Ingredients . . .

4 x 150gms (5.3oz) veal sweetbreads

4 langoustines, peeled & cooked

4 braised shallots, base cut to stay flat

250gms (8.8oz) strong flour

4 large egg yolks

1 whole egg

10ml (0.4fl.oz) olive oil infused with saffron thread

20gms (0.70oz) haggis

1 bulb raw beetroot, diced

200ml (7.3fl.oz) port wine

400ml (14.5fl.oz) clear chicken stock

1/2 turnip (pureed & drained in cheese cloth over night)

160gms (5.6oz) floury mashed potato

2gms (0.1oz) chopped chives

Pinch fresh truffle (diced)

1 recipe for creamed savoy cabbage with caraway seed

1 recipe for tomato concasse

4 sprigs of Chervil

2gms (0.1oz) Sevruga caviar

## Method . . .

To make the raviolis . . .

Blend all the pasta ingredients together in food processor until they form a tight ball. Remove & knead thoroughly on floured work surface, wrap in cling film & refrigerate until use. Roll out 1/3 pasta gradually down from the thickest to the thinnest setting on your pasta machine. Place a small amount of haggis, 5g spaced 2 inches apart using one half length of pasta, gently brush around the haggis with cold water & fold the other half to enclose the filling. Gently push down around the filling ensuring all air bubbles are pushed out. Cut each ravioli out using fluted cutter and reserve. To serve, blanch in boiling salted water for 2 mins .

For the beetroot & port wine emulsion . . .

Sweat the diced beetroot in a little olive oil without colouring, add the Port wine & reduce the liquid by half. Add the chicken stock and cook until beetroot is tender. Blend in the food processor & pass through chinoise (or fine sieve), add correct seasoning and reserve.

For the "Neeps & Tatties" cake . . .

Combine the potato & swede mix, incorporate the egg yolk, truffle & chives and season to taste. Use 2 inch stainless steal rings to form 4 potato cakes - dust with seasoned flour & pan fry in olive oil until golden brown.

To assemble the dish . . .

Warm shallots & potato cakes through in oven (170°C, 340°F) for 10 mins. Meantime pan fry sweetbreads and langoustines & blanch raviolis in boiling water for 2 minutes. Garnish shallots with tomato concasse, caviar & chervil sprig. Heat creamed cabbage & beetroot emulsion. Place cabbage on plate topped with sweetbread & top with ravioli. Place potato cake & sauce around. Serves 4.

Iain Jurgensen
Executive Chef

St Andrews Bay Hotel, St Andrews, KY16 8PN, Scotland

Tel: +44 (0) 1334 837000 · Web: www.standrewsbay.com

ST ANDREWS BAY

HAGGIS *Recipe Book*

HAGGIS *Recipe Book*

*Vegetarian Selection*

# Vegetarian Selection

## Ingredients . . .

3 mixed sweet peppers

3 large tomatoes

6 mushrooms

425gms (15oz) vegetarian haggis

2 tablespoons of tomato puree

Vegetable oil

## Method . . .

Halve and de-seed peppers, destalk mushrooms, cut top from tomatoes, scoop out (keep and set aside).

Place scooped out tomato in food processor with puree, pass through sieve after mixing and spoon blend with haggis. Fill peppers, tomatoes and mushrooms with mixture.

Brush with vegetable oil and cover with tin foil before baking in oven at 200°C (390°F). Bake peppers for 1 hour, and tomatoes and mushrooms for 30 minutes.

*Ann Stahly*

*Home Cooked Delights*

# Traditional Scotch Dinner

## Ingredients . . .

425gms (15oz) cooked haggis

3 large turnips

Salt & pepper

8 large potatoes

50gms (1.8oz) butter

2 tablespoons of olive oil

## Method . . .

Prepare the haggis until piping hot.

For the potatoes . . .

Peel the potatoes, cut into quarters and place in a pan with some salt. Bring to the boil then simmer gently until tender, remove from the heat, and drain away the water.

Leave the potatoes to dry for a couple of minutes, add the butter and olive oil, then, mash together with a fork leaving bits and pieces of potatoes un-mashed. Season well and serve.

For the turnip . . .

Peel the turnip thoroughly, remembering to take off all the outside skin, roughly chop and place in a pan of cold water with some salt.

Bring to the boil and simmer gently until tender. Drain the water away and leave to dry for a few minutes. Mash the turnip as the potatoes, remembering to leave the mixture a little lumpy, season well and serve. The reason that we leave the potatoes and the turnip like this and not completely mashed dates back to olden times when they didn't have the implements we have today to make them completely lump free.

To serve . . .

Arrange each mixture and serve as per photograph. Serves 4.

Kevin Clark
Executive Chef

*Old Course Hotel, Golf Resort & Spa, St Andrews, KY16 9SP, Scotland*
*Tel: +44 (0) 1334 474371 · Web: www.oldcoursehotel.co.uk*

OLD COURSE HOTEL
ST ANDREWS
GOLF RESORT & SPA

# HAGGIS *Recipe Book*

# HAGGIS *Recipe Book*

*Cocktail Haggis*

# Cocktail Haggis

## Ingredients . . .

230gms (8.1oz) haggis

1 tablespoon whisky (optional)

128gms (4.5oz) battermix (1pkt)

195ml (7fl.oz) water, to mix battermix

60gms (2.2oz) plain flour

1 egg

Breadcrumbs

Vegetable oil for frying

## Method . . .

Place haggis in a bowl and mix in the whisky. Roll mixture into small balls (approximately 20). Dust with flour and place in fridge for 1 hour.

Mix battermix with the egg and water and pass the haggis balls through batter and then breadcrumbs. Return to fridge until firm.

Heat oil in deep fat fryer and cook for 30 seconds until crisp which can then be eaten hot or cold. Ideal with pre-dinner drinks or as an addition to a finger buffet.

*Ann Stahly*

*Home Cooked Delights*

# HAGGIS *Recipe Book*

*Gateau of Haggis*

# Gateau Of Haggis

## Ingredients . . .

2 potatoes

Double cream to taste

60gms (2.1oz) turnip

100gms (3.5oz) haggis

10ml (0.4fl.oz) veal jus

10gms (0.35oz) butter

3ml (0.1fl.oz) single malt whisky

Picked chervil

## Method . . .

Peel and cut potato and turnip into cylindrical shapes and steam cook until tender. Layer up a ramekin with the turnip, haggis and potato.

Warm through in oven or Bain Marie, turn out onto plate, quenelle a little turnip and place on top.

Foam up whisky sauce (veal jus, butter, double cream and whisky) and pour around before garnishing with picked chervil.

Recipe makes one Gateau, increase ingredients as required.

Andrew Hamer Executive Chef

The Gleneagles Hotel, Auchterarder, PH3 1NF, Scotland
Tel: +44 (0) 1764 662231 · Web: www.gleneagles.com

GLENEAGLES

# HAGGIS *Recipe Book*

# HAGGIS *Recipe Book*  Ground Beef and Haggis Canapes

# Ground Beef and Haggis Canapes

## Ingredients . . .

170gms (6oz) cooked ground beef

235gms (8.3oz) haggis

220gms (7.8oz) mashed potatoes

150gms (5.3oz) mashed turnip

240gms (8.5oz) puff pastry

## Method . . .

Roll out puff pastry and cut with 75cm pastry cutter. Bake blind at 220°C (430°F), until golden brown. Once cold, place in ground beef and then haggis.

Pipe round about with potato and add the mashed turnip to finish.

Mixture creates approximately 16 canapes that can be served hot or cold.

*Ann Stahly*

*Home Cooked Delights*

HAGGIS *Recipe Book*

*Fillet of Scottish Beef,*
*Balmoral Style*

# Fillet of Scottish Beef, Balmoral Style

## Ingredients . . .

4 x 125gms (4.4oz) trimmed fillets of beef

150gms (5.3oz) haggis

50gms (1.8oz) thyme

50gms (1.8oz) breadcrumbs

50gms (1.8oz) unsalted butter

2 egg yolks

12 peeled baby Turnips

200gms (7.1oz) mashed potatoes

1 glass red wine

275ml (10fl.oz) beef stock

50gms (1.8oz) butter

## Method . . .

Melt 50gms (1.8oz) butter, add breadcrumbs, thyme leaves and egg yolks. Mix together. Press between 2 pieces of grease-proof paper until 5mm thick. Place in fridge to set.

Cook the turnip in salted water.

In a hot pan, season and seal the steaks. Cook in a hot oven at 180°C (360°F) for 8 minutes. Remove from oven and allow to rest. Swill out pan with wine and beef stock. When it starts to thicken, whisk in 50 gms (1.8oz) butter - this will thicken it more. Taste and check seasoning.

Warm Haggis and place on top of steak. Cut out herb and bread crust with a round cutter same size as steak. Place back in oven for 2 minutes.

Drain turnip and dry.

To serve . . .

Place steak in centre of plate. Place 3 turnips around the plate, pipe mash potatoes in between turnip, pour sauce around the plate and serve.

Enjoy with a glass of red wine or malt whisky. Serves 4.

Jeff Bland
Executive Chef

THE BALMORAL
EDINBURGH

The Balmoral Hotel, 1 Princes Street, Edinburgh, EH2 2EQ, Scotland
Tel: +44 (0) 131 5562414 · Web: www.roccofortehotels.com

HAGGIS *Recipe Book*

HAGGIS *Recipe Book*

*Haggis Jacobean*

# Haggis Jacobean

## Ingredients . . .

425gms (15oz) haggis

6 tablespoons whisky

Cream to top

## Method . . .

Divide haggis into 6 ramekin dishes. Place in oven or microwave until piping hot. Remove and add 1 tablespoon of whisky to each dish and add a swirl of cream.

Serve instantly. This makes an excellent starter to a meal.

Serves 6.

*Ann Stahly*

*Home Cooked Delights*

# Haggis Mille Feuille

## Ingredients . . .

425gms (15oz) haggis

100gms (3.5oz) black pudding

50gms (1.8oz) pre-sliced thin pancetta

60gms (2.1oz) leeks

50gms (1.8oz) puff pastry

150gms (5.3oz) potatoes

150gms (5.3oz) swede (turnip)

50ml (1.8fl.oz) scotch whisky

100ml (3.7fl.oz) fresh double cream

25gms (0.9oz) onion

2.5g (0.1oz) seasoning

## Method . . .

Pre-heat oven to 180°C (360°F). Firstly trim leeks up and wash. Cut into thin julienne strips. Wash again, dry with a cloth, mix some salt and a little olive oil, place on a tray and dry out in a warmer drawer in the oven.

Lay the strips of pancetta out onto a tray and bake in oven until they become crisp. Form the haggis into rings about 2.5cm thick (you will need 2 pieces per portion). Slice the black pudding into rings but you will only need one per portion. Peel and cook potatoes and make a very dry mash. Prepare the swede (turnip) in the same manner obviously keeping them separate.
Place the whisky, cream and a knob of butter into a saucepan, heat until sauce becomes thick, take off, and leave to one side.

Using stainless steel rings of about 6.4cm diameter and approximately 5.1cm in depth assemble the dish with the black pudding as a base, haggis, swede (turnip), haggis and potato. Once they are all in rings place onto a baking tray and cook for 30 minutes in the oven.
Cut out rings of puff pastry to fit the top of the haggis mille feuille and cook in oven until golden brown.

To serve . . .

Place mille feuille in to the centre of the plate and top with the dried leeks and one strip of crisp pancetta, place puff pastry on top of that and spoon the cream sauce around the outside of the haggis. Serves 6.

Paul Newman Executive Chef

Caledonian Hotel, 4 Princes St, Edinburgh, EH1 2AB, Scotland
Tel: +44 (0) 131 2228888 · Web: www.hilton.com/caledonian

Caledonian Hilton

HAGGIS *Recipe Book*

**HAGGIS** *Recipe Book*

*Baked Potato with Scotch Haggis*

# Baked Potato with Scotch Haggis

## Ingredients . . .

1 large baking potato
90gms (3.2oz) haggis
25gms (0.88oz) butter

## Method . . .

Spike potato with a fork and place in microwave for 12 minutes or wrap in tin foil and place in oven at 200°C (390°F) for 1 hour. Remove and split, add butter and gently fork in and add the haggis. Serve hot.

Recipe makes one potato, increase ingredients as required.

*Ann Stahly*

*Home Cooked Delights*

HAGGIS *Recipe Book*

Fillet of Angus Beef, Turnip Fondant,
Pomme Purée and Haggis Cannelloni

# Fillet of Angus Beef, Turnip Fondant, Pomme Puree and Haggis Cannelloni

## Ingredients . . .

4 fillets of Angus beef

170gms (6oz) haggis
(room temperature)

Dark green of one small leek

4 turnip discs (fondants)

850ml (31.2fl.oz) vegetable stock

16 peeled and roasted shallots

16 peeled & blanched baby carrots

16 peeled & blanched asparagus spears

Wild mushrooms

4 medium sized potatoes
(for pomme puree)

250gms (8.8oz) unsalted butter

4 sprigs of chervil

280ml (10.3fl.oz) madeira sauce (made
from veal stock and reduced madeira)

## Method . . .

For the Turnip Fondant . . .

Line a saucepan with diced butter and place fondants on top. Cover with vegetable stock and cook for 20 minutes, reduce the stock and colour the turnip base golden brown.

For the pomme puree . . .

Place the potatoes in a saucepan and cover with cold water. Add 1 tablespoon of salt, bring to the boil and simmer until tender. Drain off and place in vegetable mill, puree then pass through a fine sieve. Beat in the butter and season to taste.

For the cannelloni . . .

Blanche the leeks in boiling water for about 1 minute, remove and instantly cool in ice water, drain and pat dry. Place the leek on a sqaure piece of cling film and season with salt & pepper. Place about 3 tablespoons of haggis on top and roll into a sausage shape, twisting the cling film at both ends to secure. Repeat 3 more times to make 4 cannelloni's. Reheat in a steamer for 6-8 minutes or in a pan of simmering water.

To complete the dish . . .

Heat a little oil and clarified butter in a sauce pan until almost smoking, then add the beef fillets, season and seal on both sides. Place in a hot oven and cook for about 8-10 minutes. When cooked remove and allow to rest.

Assemble the dishes as per photograph. Serves 4.

Paul Whitecross,
Executive Chef

Carnoustie Golf Hotel and Resort Ltd, The Links, Carnoustie, DD7 7JE, Scotland

Tel: +44 (0) 1241 411999 · Web: www.carnoustie-hotel.com

CARNOUSTIE

HAGGIS *Recipe Book*

**HAGGIS** *Recipe Book*

*Scottish Pumpkin Pie*

# Scottish Pumpkin Pie

## Ingredients . . .

2 x 23cm cooked shortcrust
flan cases

500gms (18oz) haggis

500gms (18oz) pumpkin puree

275ml (10fl.oz) fresh cream

3 eggs

150gms (5.3oz) caster sugar

1/2 tablespoon salt

Grated peel of large lemon

1 tablespoon ground ginger

1/2 tablespoon ground cloves

1/2 tablespoon ground cinnamon

## Method . . .

1/2 fill pastry cases with haggis and set aside.

Make puree by cutting pumpkin into chunks, removing skin and seeds, boil in lightly salted water until tender, drain and put through sieve. Set aside.

Beat cream lightly with eggs, lemon peel and sugar. Stir mixture into pumpkin puree, add salt, ginger, cinnamon and cloves. Mix well then spoon over haggis, filling case full.

Bake at 180°C (360°F) until set and golden brown, approximately 1 1/4 hours.

This dish can be served hot or cold and as a starter or a desert.

*Ann Stahly*

*Home Cooked Delights*

**HAGGIS** *Recipe Book*

*Corn Fed Chicken with Haggis,*
*Bashed Neeps and Champit Tatties*

# Corn Fed Chicken with Haggis, Bashed Neeps and Champit Tatties

## Ingredients . . .

4 x 175gms (6.2oz) corn fed
Chicken supremes

300gms (10.6oz) haggis

200gms (7.1oz) turnip puree

200gms potato puree

200gms parsnip puree

8 baby carrots (blanched)

8 asparagus spears (blanched)

4 sprigs of thyme

20gms (0.7oz) butter

Malt whisky jus:

60gms (2.1oz) butter

50gms (1.8oz) chopped vegetables

60ml (2.2fl.oz) malt whisky

1ltr (36.4fl.oz) brown stock

## Method . . .

Stuff chicken supremes with haggis, season and roll in tin foil into sausage shaped cylinders, cook in hot oven 200°C (390°F) for 14-16 minutes, leave to rest, then slice in even slices.

Put the warm seasoned potato and turnip puree into two separate piping bags, cut off ends and then carefully put the two piping bags into one more. This will let you pipe the two purees at the same time giving good visual impact.

Warm the baby carrots and asparagus in boiling salted water, then toss in butter. Warm parsnip puree and quenelle with two large dessert spoons. Warm malt whisky jus and assemble dish as per photograph.

For the malt whisky jus . . .

Melt 30g (1.1oz) of butter in a thick bottomed pan, then add the chopped vegetables and cook gently for 2-3 minutes. Next, add malt whisky and flambé. Add brown stock and reduce by two thirds. Finally remove from the heat, season and whisk in the remaining butter and keep warm without boiling.

Serves 4.

Colin Watson
Executive Chef

THE WESTIN TURNBERRY RESORT
SCOTLAND

The Westin Turnberry Resort, Turnberry, Ayrshire, KA26 9LT, Scotland
Tel: +44 (0) 1655 331000 · Web: www.westin.com/turnberry

HAGGIS *Recipe Book*

HAGGIS *Recipe Book*

*Haggis Wrapped Venison Medalions, with Savoy Potatoes*

# Haggis Wrapped Venison Medalions, with Savoy Potatoes

## Ingredients . . .

1/2 loin of venison (larder trimmed)

425gms (15oz) haggis

Some crépinette/caul to wrap the venison

250gms (8.8oz) butter

Salt & pepper

1 large onion, finely sliced

Fresh chopped thyme

4 medium potatoes, peeled and sliced

550ml (20fl.oz) chicken stock

1.1ltr (40fl.oz) venison stock

1 large glass red wine

6 finely chopped shallots

4 portions of Spinach, picked & washed

1 pinch sugar

117cm tartlet moulds

## Method . . .

For the sauce . . .

In a sauce pan, reduce the red wine and shallots to a glaze, then add the venison stock and reduce to 275ml (10fl.oz) volume. Strain and keep to the side.

For the potatoes . . .

Fry the sliced onion with the chopped thyme, salt, pepper, sugar and butter until golden brown and soft. Arrange layers of potato and onion mixture in the tartlet moulds until filled - the top layer should be potato. Cover with a knob of butter and fill with chicken stock. Cook in a pre-heated oven at 160°C (320°F) until golden brown and all the stock has been absorbed.

For the venison . . .

In a hot pan seal and brown the venison but do not overcook it. Allow to drain on kitchen paper. Top the venison with a generous amount of haggis and then wrap in the caul to hold it together. Next re-seal the venison and place in the oven for 12 minutes or until cooked medium rare. Take out and allow the meat to rest for 3 minutes before carving into medallions.

To serve . . .

Wilt the spinach and divide on to the dinner plates, then place a potato cake on top. Serve 3 venison medallions on each potato with the red wine sauce and add garnish.

Serves 4.

*Craig Rowland*

Craig Rowland Executive Chef

Skibo Castle, Dornoch, IV25 3RQ, Scotland

Tel: +44 (0) 1862 894600 · Web: www.carnegieclub.co.uk

The Cam Sron
AGED 14 YEARS
in selected sherry casks

Speyside Single Malt
Scotch Whisky

GEORGIAN

Distilled and Bottled in Scotland
Inverarity Vaults Ltd., Edinburgh, Scotland    40% vol

HAGGIS *Recipe Book*

*Haggis Spring Rolls, with Sweet Potato
and Ginger, Blackberry and Whisky Ju*